RELAXATION

The Relaxation Remedy for Anxiety

By

Vicki Joy

Other Books by Vicki Joy

ACNE: Natural Acne Scar Treatments for Clear Skin
http://amzn.to/29WlzA4

ANTI-AGING: The Anti-Aging Guide to Healthy Skin and the Fountain of Youth
http://amzn.to/1Q1P5CU

ANXIETY: Getting Free From Fear And Panic Attacks
http://amzn.to/1Thj2uS

ARTHRITIS: How to Relieve and Reverse Rheumatoid Arthritis Today
http://amzn.to/2a8bmLf

ASTHMA: How To Get Asthma Free Naturally
http://amzn.to/1Q8f6kj

FOCUS: The Key to Success
http://amzn.to/1rQsG0H

INTROVERT: How To Use The Introvert Advantage And Introvert Power
http://amzn.to/1XV8WH9

Unstoppable You! How to Build Your Confidence and Go After the Life of Your Dreams
http://amzn.to/2hhpwSw

WEIGHT LOSS - The Mindfulness Diet
http://amzn.to/1V6XMN7

This document is geared towards providing exact and reliable information in regards to the topic and issue covered. The publication is sold with the idea that the publisher is not required to render accounting, officially permitted, or otherwise, qualified services. If advice is necessary, legal or professional, a practiced individual in the profession should be ordered.

- From a Declaration of Principles which was accepted and approved equally by a Committee of the American Bar Association and a Committee of Publishers and Associations.

The information herein is offered for informational purposes solely, and is universal as so. The presentation of the information is without contract or any type of guarantee assurance.

The trademarks that are used are without any consent, and the publication of the trademark is without permission or backing by the trademark owner. All trademarks and brands within this book are for clarifying purposes only and are the owned by the owners themselves, not affiliated with this document.

Table of Contents

Introduction

Chapter 1: What is Relaxation?

Chapter 2: Natural Ways Relax and Calm Anxiety

Chapter 3: Relaxation Techni□ues for Anxiety

Chapter 4: Have a Go-To Relaxation Techni□ue

Chapter 5: Managing Anxiety With Relaxation Techni□ues

Chapter 6: Benefits of Relaxation and Techniques

Conclusion

Introduction

Thank you for purchasing *"RELAXATION - The Relaxation Remedy for Anxiety!"* This book contains proven strategies on how to use simple everyday relaxation methods to release anxiety and stress.

One method is *progressive relaxation exercises*, which re uire an awareness of the tension in your body's muscles, and an awareness of the opposite state of relaxation. Knowing and recognizing the difference allows you to slowly learn how to control the level of tension in your body. What's wonderful about progressive relaxation exercise is that, once you become skilled at it, you will be able to switch into relaxation mode with ease. You will be able to determine where there is tension in your body, and then to target those areas with relaxation exercises. Progressive relation works by having you relax your entire body in sequence using a variety of different thought processes and methods.

Another method is *relaxation response*, which is similar to progressive relaxation, but does not require the initial awareness of tension in your muscles. According to the American Psychological Association, relaxation response is "a physical state of deep rest that changes a person's physical and emotional responses to stress".

Both methods are very effective in releasing anxiety and stress, and in bringing the body back into a balanced state of relaxation. Which type of exercise you choose will simply depend on what you are most comfortable with. Choose the method that works best for you, and enjoy the benefits of relaxation!

Chapter 1: What is Relaxation?

We talk a lot about stress in our society, but very little about relaxation – the antidote for stress and anxiety. Odd, isn't it? The ability to relax is, in my view, undervalued. We seem to place more value on people who appear to be driven, achievers, go-getters. "He's a bit laid-back" is more likely to be an insult than a compliment!

We all need to relax more, as we all encounter and experience stress in many different aspects. *Relaxation is defined as "the state of being free from tension and anxiety".* The everyday tensions of life can sometimes weigh too heavily on us, crushing our sense of joy and well-being. The friction we experience in interpersonal encounters can damage even the best of relationships, causing undue stress and anxiety.

The ideal image of the truly relaxed person is that of a sprinter tearing down the track. Watch his face - see how the skin ripples easily. He's utterly relaxed, even to his facial muscles. He's pumping his arms, but again, see how the muscles float freely. Relaxed. Not holding him back. Now look at his eyes. They're focused on one thing only - the finish line. This is the paradox of relaxation: *we perform optimally when we are both relaxed and focused.*

This is the formula for success that is applicable to every aspect of life. Relaxation + focus = optimal performance. In social relationships. At work. In sports and athletics. It's the goal of every sports psychologist - to help their athletes stay in control of body and mind, even during the most challenging performances. It's called being "in the zone" – allowing and confident knowing that practice and preparation will kick in and do their job. Watch a top-flight journalist or anchorperson at work reporting an epic breaking news story and you will see what I mean. Relaxation + focus is the difference between competence and mastery, and make even the most challenging circumstances seem easy.

How do we get "in the zone"? How can we apply this formula of *relaxation + focus = optimal results* in our everyday lives? Relaxation is a crucial component in this equation, since it is extremely difficult to be focused if we are feeling anxiety or stress. The goal here is to be able to bring the body back into a relaxed state whenever we start to feel anxiety or stress. Dr. Herbert Benson, founder of Harvard's Mind/Body Medical Institute, describes bringing the body back into a relaxed state as 'Relaxation Response'. According to Psychology today, Relaxation Response is defined as "your personal ability to encourage your body to release chemicals and brain signals that make your muscles and organs slow down and increase blood flow to the brain".

Let me suggest a few simple techniques which you can use, without special training or expense, to help you relax, and shed some of your daily load of anxiety and stress.

The first techni☐ue is the simplest: just take a deep breath in, hold it, and release slowly. As you release, let your shoulders drop. You'd be surprised how much tension resides in our shoulders. A variation of this techni☐ue is the walking meditation. As you walk along, count your paces. Breath in for 5 paces, hold for 5, breathe out for 5. Start again. You can vary the numbers to find what works best for you.

Another useful, everyday techni☐ue is to develop awareness of your body. For example, observe your breathing. Become aware of the breath entering your body. Notice the slight increase in tension in your chest muscles as your chest expands. The release of tension on the outbreath. Any part of your body can be treated in this way. Pay close attention to your body in the present moment, and you will rapidly shed some of your tension.

A third approach is to use an external object, any object, as your focus. A cup, for example. Let everything else disappear from your attention and focus exclusively on the cup. Become aware of its glaze. The porcelain beneath. Sense its curvature. When you focus intently on an everyday object, allowing that object to fill your field of awareness, all other worries and stress dissipate and disappear, allowing you to experience a moment of true relaxation.

Chapter 2: Natural Ways Relax and Calm Anxiety

Anxiety is a natural part of life - so natural that every person has experienced some form of anxiety. There are people who experience sporadic episodes of anxiety, and others who experience anxiety on most days of their life. While there are medications that can curb anxiety, most of these medications have harmful side effects.

The good news is that most people don't always need medication to address anxiety and stress. These maladies can often be effectively managed and remedied with all-natural techniqes, with no harmful side effects. There are simple natural methods of relaxing the mind and body to control the symptoms of irritability, nervousness, lack of concentration and fear that make up the anxiety response. Of course, it is always important to follow your doctor's advice when it comes to dealing with any type of anxiety conditions.

Anxiety in its more severe forms can often be debilitating, and can significantly impact the quality of your everyday life. It can cause overwhelming feelings of nervousness and fear that can affect your enjoyment of life and family, as well as your performance at work. It can also cause undue stress, which comes with its own set of problems – both physiological and physical. It is important to pinpoint the source or sources of your anxiety (i.e., stressors). Once identified, these stressors should be eliminated, or curbed as much as possible.

With the increased pressures of modern life more and more people find it difficult to switch off and relax at the end of the day. This can lead to sleepless nights, which creates further anxiety that can make life feel more unbearable. Seeking out natural methods to lower your anxiety and stress levels is important, as these natural methods can be used everyday by practically anyone, without the harmful side effects of many medications. There are several natural techniques to choose from, a few of which I will mention below. The important thing is to take the time to take care of yourself, find the techniques that work for you, and implement them in your daily life.

Following are great techniques you can use to safely and naturally reduce the anxiety and stress in your life. These natural techniques may be used to address any level of stress or anxiety – from mild to severe; or from sporadic to chronic.

Get plenty of sleep - A good night's sleep can restore your energy, and can reset your anxiety to a much more manageable level. Some people may wake up anxious from a disturbing dream, or because they have not managed to release the anxious energy from the preceding day. Others may wake up already stressed out because they have an anxiety-producing event to face later that day, or because they have been dealing with an ongoing stressful situation. When you get a good night's sleep, you awake refreshed and ready for the day. You are better equipped to face the day, regardless of what comes.

Practice daily meditation - Meditation is "spend[ing] time in quiet thought for ... relaxation" (merriam-webster.com/dictionary). It is the art of using your breath and your mind to relax your body and release nervous energy. In the beginning, you will want to find a quiet place to sit or lie down. Close your eyes and focus on the natural in and out of your breath. Vocalize a soft mantra, or affirmation, which can be a syllable, a word, or a phrase like, "relax, relax", "ohm", or something like "I am calm and relaxed." Use your mind and breath to gradually relax all the muscles of the body, especially those muscles that are tense from stress and anxiety. Remain focused on your breath and on relaxing your body for several minutes, allowing the release of negative, anxious energy from your body. When you are fully relaxed, stay in that state for a few more minutes so you can feel the relaxation happen. Practicing mediation on a daily basis can go a long way to lowering anxiety and stress levels.

Tai Chi - This is "a Chinese martial art and form of stylized, meditative exercise, characterized by methodically slow circular and stretching movements and positions of bodily balance" (dictionary.com). It involves standing and moving through different poses that require your intense focus. It looks a lot like a dance that involves your breath and your muscles, and flows from one pose to another in a natural way. The Mayo Clinic describes tai chi as "meditation in motion", and as "a gentle way to fight stress". Tai chi is an effective method for reducing the anxiety and stress experienced in daily life. Tai Chi classes are offered in many community centers. In warmer climates or seasons, it is also common to see groups of people practicing outdoors – especially in parks. As always, it is advisable to check with your doctor before starting an exercise program.

Yoga - Yoga is a spiritual and physical discipline that originated in the Far East. It involves focusing on controlling the breath, meditation, and specific poses. Yoga has spread worldwide, with millions practicing it on a regular basis. In fact, yoga is purported to have more than 50 different health benefits, one of which is the ability to elicit the relaxation response in the body and subsequently lower anxiety. There are many types of yoga. Some are more relaxing, while others are more energizing. One of the relaxing types of yoga is the popular Hatha yoga, which is ideal for anxiety and stress relief. Hatha yoga guides you through different poses in a smooth and natural way. It uses breath work that controls the speed and length of time spent in poses, and is extremely beneficial in helping to reduce both stress and anxiety.

Mindfulness - Psychology Today describes mindfulness as the "state of active, open attention on the present". It's the art of focusing on the here and now, of going about your day with your focus being on the present moment, and on the ordinary aspects of life. When we do things mindfully, we engage our senses in such a way that keeps us fully engaged in the present time; thereby spending less time worrying about the future, or about upcoming anxiety-producing events. Learning to live "in the moment" is an art that takes practice, but is well worth the effort because of its effectiveness in reducing both stress and anxiety.

Visualization – this is a type of meditation that allows the mind to go somewhere else, and away from anxiety-provoking situations. In visualization, you spend time mentally traveling to a place that you find calming and relaxing. For some people, this might be hiking up a mountain with spectacular views. For others, it might be a sandy beach in Barbados, or tending a beautiful garden. I call this exercise "living in my imagination". After spending several minutes in your imagined place of serenity and comfort, you will be able to face the challenges of life feeling much better and calmer. With practice, the ability to visualize can become second nature. The beauty of this method is that it can be practiced at anytime and anywhere – even in the midst of a chaotic situation. It creates a peaceful mental space that allows you to pause, take a breath, and put things in proper perspective.

Regular Exercise – While the physical benefits of exercise are pretty well known, exercise is also beneficial for emotional and psychological well-being, going a long way toward reducing anxiety and stress. According to the Anxiety and Depression Association of America "exercise and other physical activity produce endorphins—chemicals in the brain that act as natural painkillers—and also improve the ability to sleep, which in turn reduces stress". Strength training, or aerobic exercises such as cycling, running, walking or swimming, will get your heart rate going, releasing nervous energy as you exercise. You may finish with a sense of fatigue plus an "exercise euphoria" that will alleviate anxious thoughts. It is always recommended that you consult a medical professional before beginning an exercise regimen.

Regular massages - We all know about the reputed benefits of a massage in aiding relaxation of the body and mind. Whilst you could get a partner or close friend to give your shoulders, back or feet a good rub down, to truly feel long-term benefits you should enlist the services of a trained professional to give you regular massages. Don't think of this as an indulgent treat but rather an essential part of your well-being routine. For as well as relaxing the muscles, the benefits of regular massage include improved blood flow and a boosted immune system.

Hang up your phone - When you leave the office you need to be able to switch off from work, and that includes your phone! This is important to do as once your work colleagues get into the habit of being able to contact you at all hours they will. Remember, the phone is there for your convenience, not just the caller's.

Compile some chillout tunes - Put together or buy a CD of relaxing music to ease your mind and help you switch off from the outside world. Research has shown that even during gestation, relaxing/classical music can be beneficial in promoting well-being.

Read a good book - Emily Dickinson wrote, "There is not frigate like a book to take us lands away," which is a great way to sum up the way in which reading a good book can help you to get your mind off your worries.

Chapter 3: Relaxation Techni☐ues for Anxiety

Problems with stress and anxiety are becoming increasingly common. The need for relaxation cannot be overemphasized. Engagements in daily problems can tie your emotions, nerves and body into knots. Constant strains like this can have long term effects on your quality of life. You can develop ulcers, and a host of other physical problems. It can effect the nerves, cause you to have a negative attitude, and wreck havoc on your health.

The stress is multiplied if you have a difficult supervisor, or work in an unpleasant environment. Constant pressure can cause loss of sleep, appetite, and other functions. Having a job you are not suited to accentuates the problem. We all have different abilities and temperaments. It is best for you and your employer if you have a job that suits your ability, ways of thinking, and doing things. If the job fits, your tasks will be natural for you to do

.

Some symptoms of anxiety include:
- Difficulty breathing;
- Feeling as though you can't get enough air;
- Racing heartbeat;
- Feeling dizzy, lightheaded;

- Experiencing a feeling of dread;
- Nausea;
- Trembling, shaking or sweating;
- Feeling nervous;
- Feeling extremely stressed;
- Experiencing a sense of paralyzing fear;
- Hot flashes;
- Sudden chills;
- Choking sensation;
- Chest pains;
- Tingling in the fingers or toes; or
- A fear that you are dying or going crazy.

It is important to understand that relaxation techniques work best when used over time. Generally, they will not provide instantaneous relief of anxiety or stress symptoms. This is why it is important to use them on a regular basis. Ideally, in fact, the practice of relaxation techniques should become part of your daily life. In addition, most people find that these techni ues work best when you make a point of practicing them when you are feeling calm and not stressed.

If left untreated, stress can affect the body in a number of ways. Stress usually results in tense muscles. This in turn can lead to issues with posture, or aches and pain all over the body. An effective strategy for reducing the feelings of stress and anxiety is to work on reducing the tension in the muscles to bring the body into a more relaxed state. This chapter offers a couple relaxation methods for reducing stress and anxiety – *instant relaxation,* or *deep relaxation methods.* These techniques may be practiced almost anywhere at any time to help release stress and loosen up the body.

Instant Relaxation Methods

Instant relaxation methods are ideal for quick relief. They require very little time, and may be practiced anywhere at anytime. Begin by focusing on the areas of your body that feel are tense, for example, shoulder, back or neck muscles. Once you are focusing on the tense muscles, you may start relaxing them one-by-one. The best means to achieve this relaxation technique is to intentionally tense and release the muscles for brief periods – say for five seconds at a time.

Another is a simple breathing technique which may be practiced while sitting or standing. Begin with your head held upright and facing forward. Now focus on taking short deep breaths. This helps in relaxing the muscles and resetting your focus on your breath, and way from anxiety-producing thoughts.

For instant relaxation, you may also try rubbing your hand over your forehead gently. This gentle massage is intended to relaxed the "frown muscles" that tense up as a sign of stress. As you gently massage the forehead, you'll notice that the creased lines formed as a result of frowning will slowly release and fade away.

Deep Relaxation

Deep relaxation focuses on "quieting the mind in order to create inner peace and better health" (Psychology Today). It employs both physical and mental exercises to achieve this objective. This technique has long been used to help people who suffer with anxiety disorder, depression, or stress related ailments. During the state of deep relaxation, the release of stress chemicals into the bloodstream is significantly reduced, and the impact of stress chemicals on the body is drastically alleviated.

Unlike instant relaxation, deep relaxation may not be practiced anytime and anywhere, as it requires a longer period of uninterrupted time in a calm quiet location. It is best applied after an especially difficult day, or in preparation for a particularly stressful upcoming event.

To benefit from the deep relaxation technique, you should to find a quiet location, where you can be guaranteed at least 20 – 30 minutes of uninterrupted time. Be sure to turn off all devices (eg. cellphones, laptops, TVs etc.), and remove or cover any objects that may cause you to become distracted.

Ideally, this environment should also be neat and clean, with no reflective surfaces. It is okay to have soothing music playing very softly in the background. The goal here is to create a space that is conducive to silencing your mind, thereby enabling you to achieve deep relaxation.

To practice the deep relaxation techni ue, begin by taking off your shoes, and wearing loose comfortable clothing. You may lie flat on your back, or sit on a comfortable chair or floor mat. Close your eyes and take deep breaths. As you inhale deeply, bring your awareness to each part of your body. As you exhale, allow that body part to completely relax – releasing all tension. To help the mind to focus on relaxing the body, you should just focus on your breath and on each body part. For example, as I inhale, I think "I am now fully aware of my forehead", and as I exhale, I think "my forehead is now completely relaxed", and so on as I would my way throughout my body just focused on my breath and on completely relaxing each part of my body.

Chapter 4: Have a Go-To Relaxation Technique

What do you do when your mind is running like an endless loop video that you can't shut off, your muscles are tense, and your worries are putting on a parade that would rival any holiday extravaganza? Having an arsenal of stress-reducing tools, and routine relaxation exercises is the answer. When we are stressed and feel ready to explode, our muscles tense up, our heart rate accelerates, our breathing increases, and our brain sends a rush of cortisol (stress hormone) into our blood stream. This is the body's "fight or flight" mechanism, and if its release is prolonged, it has negative effects on our psychological and physical well being.

The Relaxation Response is the antidote to the 'fight or flight' response. Consciously and intentionally employing a relaxation response through a variety of relaxation techniques will help bring your body into balance, and reduce the stress that can cause anxiety.

It is important to determine which relaxation techniques you will use, and become well acquainted with how to practice this technique before you experience anxiety and stress. If you frequently have issues with anxiety at work, try to find a quiet place where you can go and have 5 to 10 minutes without interruption, even if it's to your car. You want a quiet environment, something to focus on (a soothing sound, an object, a thought), a comfortable position, and a passive attitude. The purpose is to interrupt the negative thought process or influence.

A quiet environment is important to help maintain focus on bringing your mind and body into a relaxed state. Breathing is a good focal point, as it has the double benefit of helping you relax while assuring a good oxygen to the bloodstream. Inhale deeply through your nose, then slowly exhale through your mouth.

A comfortable position will also help in relaxing the muscles, which will in turn aid in clearing the mind. Muscle tension is a large component of anxiety. When you are in a comfortable position, you can better concentrate on relaxing all your muscle groups. Find your quiet place, find your focus, and then concentrate on consciously relaxing the muscles in your body in concert with your deep breathing excercise.

A passive attitude – an attitude on 'non resistance' - is one of the most important components to achieving a relaxed state, and to handling anxiety. It is an effective tool for dealing with challenging situations, and is especially effective when you feel your stress and anxiety levels mounting. Even if you can't escape to your place of relaxation, a passive attitude can carry you through a day that is full of stress and anxiety.

Do you know the Serenity Prayer? "Grant me the serenity to accept the things I cannot change, the courage to change the things I can, and the wisdom to know the difference." In short, become an expert at identifying the things you cannot change, then make "oh, well!" your personal mantra. This is not a cop-out of any kind! When you really think about it, what is the point of getting upset over things that you have no control over,nor ability to change?

If you make a mistake, learn from it. You'll be more careful next time. "Oh, well" will help you let go of stress and anxiety associated with situations beyond your control, and will allow you to think more clearly as you deal with them. A passive attitude is not an invitation for others to walk all over you. On the contrary, you may find that others come to respect your ability to deal with stressful situations without being emotionally charged – of remaining 'calm in the storm'.

Think of all the situations that caused you a flood of negative emotion, and evaluate how adopting an "oh, well" attitude would have changed how you dealt with those situations. Instead of getting angry with your partner for squeezing the toothpaste from the middle of the tube, you'll buy your own tube of toothpaste. Instead of throwing the phone against the wall when you're frustrated with a difficult client, you'll calmly and politely respond that you'll get back to them. Practice balancing your stress response with a relaxation response. You'll find it reduces anxiety symptoms significantly.

Chapter 5: Managing Anxiety With Relaxation Techni☐ues

Anxiety attacks are as old as humankind, and are part of our genetic survival mechanism known as the fight or flight mechanism. Anxiety can be described as feeling nervous, overwhelmed, 'out-of-sorts' or panic. In its more severe cases, anxiety can cause a sense of crippling fear or debilitating panic attacks. So getting a handle on this condition before it has chance to become a chronic, paralyzing issue is essential to living a happy and well-balanced healthy life. Anxiety and its symptoms are often managed with prescription medication, which in many cases come with harmful side effects. Relaxation techniques on the other hand, are natural and harmless alternatives to the potentially damaging prescription drugs for addressing anxiety and its associated symptoms.

Generally speaking, relaxation techniques (the relaxation response) involve redirecting our attention to something calming, and increasing our awareness of our body in the present moment. Practicing the relaxation techniques mentioned below have been shown to offer many 'well-being' advantages including:

- reducing anger and frustration;
- lowering blood pressure;
- lowering your heart rate;

- increasing blood flow to major muscles;
- improving concentration;
- reducing nervous tension;
- alleviating muscle pain; and
- creating a general sense of wellbeing.

Autogenic relaxation: Autogenic refers to something that comes from within you. In this relaxation technique, you utilize both visual imagery and body awareness to reduce stress. You would repeat words or suggestions in your mind (e.g., peace, peace, peace.... or, breathe, breathe, breathe...) to help you relax and reduce the tension in your muscles.

Progressive muscle relaxation: This technique focuses on slowly releasing tension and then relaxing each muscle group. The objective here is to become aware of the difference between muscle tension and relaxation. The most commonly used example of this is to start by tensing and then relaxing your toes and progressively working your way up to the neck and head. Each contraction should last about 5 seconds with each relaxation lasting 30 seconds.

Visualization: Visualization involves mentally transporting yourself into a peaceful, calming place. When using visualization to manage anxiety, aim to use as many senses as possible, including smell, sight, sound, and touch, to make the visualization experience more effective. Examples are the smell of freshly baked bread, the feeling of the sun beaming down on your body, or the sound of rhythmic waves crashing on the shore.

Other common relaxation techniques include yoga, listening to music, exercise, meditation, deep breathing, and massage.

Chapter 6: Benefits of Relaxation and Techniques

Being able to relax is an important part of everyone's life. When we are relaxed, we don't get irritable and we are friendlier people to be around. Aside from this, staying calm has other benefits including improved customer service, better performance at work, the ability to boost confidence and enhancing your general positive wellbeing. In the workplace, having calm, stress free staff will increase employee engagement and allow them to respond, rather than react and see things in a clearer light, ensuring increased productivity and morale.

The use of relaxation techniques provide a number of important advantages, besides helping you to feel less stressed. For example, these techniues can help to lower your blood pressure, which can decrease your chances of having a heart attack. By reducing your stress levels your immune system will also experience a great improvement as well as your sleep patterns.

Another benefit of being stress free is that your general health is better. Your sleeping patterns become more consistent and your appetite is improved. Adapting your nutrition regimen or altering your exercise routine can also have positive effects in and out of the workplace.

Personally, I have benefitted greatly from managing anxiety with the help of relaxation techniques, and you can too. The beauty of these types of natural alternative remedies for anxiety is that they can help diffuse what feels like the ticking time bomb of anxiety whether it is spiraling out of control, or you've at least been able to temporarily get it under control. Another benefit is that basic relaxation methods are often free of cost, easy to implement, provide instantaneous relief, and and easily accessible - may be practiced by anyone at any time.

Relaxation can bring about a number of physical health benefits. During relaxation, your heart rate and breathing slows down. Your blood pressure decreases, and the blood flow to your primary muscles is increased. Chronic pain and muscle tension are also significantly reduced when practicing relaxation techniques. The body systems including the circulatory, immune, gastrointestinal, and respiratory systems also function better.

Relaxation has also been shown to improve certain health conditions. Skin disorders such as eczema, dermatitis, and psoriasis tend to improve upon relaxation. Heartburn, ulcers, asthma, emphysema, arthritis, migraine, epilepsy, premenstrual and menopausal syndromes, angina, fibromyalgia, insomnia, and diabetes mellitus are just some of the conditions which are known to improve with relaxation.

Relaxation is a way to calm the mind. People who are practicing relaxation exercises are known to get better sleep. Relaxation can also help you keep your emotions in check leading to less bouts of anger and crying spells. Furthermore, it can increase your memory, concentration, and problem solving skills. Anxiety disorders, depression, and panic attacks are also known to improve with relaxation.

Below are some relaxation techniques that help alleviate stress:

Meditate

Ease stress and anxiety with some heavy breathing. You can do this whenever you start feeling overwhelmed. Just sit up straight in a chair, feet on the floor, close your eyes and focus on your breathing. To help you control it, you can always place your hand on your stomach to control your inhaling and exhaling. Inhale through your nose and out through your mouth.

Do something you love

The next chance you get, take some time out, even if it's just an hour, to do something you love. Like reading, drawing or even just watching a film. You should always make time for some self-relaxation.

Decompress

Try placing a warm towel or other heat wrap around your neck and shoulders. Sit down, close your eyes and relax your whole top half, including your face. Stay with it there for about ten minutes and breathe deeply. This helps to release tension around the top of your back.

Go green

If you drink a lot of tea or coffee, why not try going green? Purchase some green tea, or chamomile tea and drink this throughout the day instead. Caffeine seems to increase the hormone linked with stress so try out different drinks with more health benefits. They can help improve your performance, reduce any stress you are currently under and also clear your mind.

Remember that your health and well-being areimportant, so take care of your body and mind!

Conclusion

Thank you again for downloading this book! I hope this book was helping in offering all natural, easy-to-do, everyday techniques for addressing stress and anxiety, and helping you to relax more. The aim is that we can all benefit from feeling more in control of our emotions and responses, as we confront the stressors that assail us on a daily basis.

The next step is to try out the techniques discussed in this book. Choose the ones that work best for you, and practice them regularly. The goal is to master a few relaxation techniques so that you will have them at the ready when needed.

Finally, if you found the ideas presented in this book helpful, then I'd like to ask you for a favor, Would you be kind enough to leave a review for this book on Amazon? It'd be greatly appreciated!

Thank you and best wishes!

Made in the USA
Lexington, KY
25 May 2018